British Kept Comin'
A Guide To The Battle of New Orleans
For Boys Only®

Photography by John D. Weigand
Poetry by Penelope Dyan

Bellissima Publishing, LLC
Jamul, California
www.bellissimapublishing.com

Copyright © 2014 by Penny D. Weigand and John D. Weigand

All rights reserved. No part of this book may be
reproduced or transmitted in any form or by any means,
electronic or mechanical, including photocopying,
recording, or by any other means, or by any information or
storage retrieval system, without permission from the publisher.

ISBN 978-1-61477-162-3
First Edition

"I feel in the depths of my soul that it is the highest, most sacred, and most irreversible part of my obligation to preserve the union of these states, although it may cost me my life."

Andrew Jackson
The Seventh President of the United States of America

British Kept Comin'
Bellissima Publishing, LLC

Introduction

The Battle of New Orleans (1814-1815) the last battle of the War of 1812, ended attempts of England to regain control of American Colonies that were lost in the American Revolution in the War for Independence. General Andrew Jackson, the Pirate Jean Lafitte and his men, along with local volunteers, defended the city of New Orleans! The final battle took place January 8, 1815. You can walk the breadth of the field, if you like, see the monuments and more; but the best part is what you don't see, and what you can imagine, especially if you are a boy! You can also see the plantation house of the Chalmet family, who were left in dire, financial ruin after the battles of New Orleans. They sold the house in 1817 to brothers Hilaire and Louis St. Amand, who were legally declared free people of color and allowed under the laws of Louisiana to own property as well as slaves. They repaired the house and restored the land to a sugar plantation at a time when sugar production in Louisiana was a rapidly growing industry.

Written by award winning author, attorney and former teacher, Penelope Dyan. with photographs by John D. Weigand, this 'learn to read' book is meant for boys, but girls are free to read it, of course! Look for the music video that goes with this book on the Bellissimavideo YouTube channel to further enhance the learning experience!

British Kept Comin'
Bellissima Publishing, LLC

British Kept Comin'
A Guide To The Battle of New Orleans
For Boys Only ®

Photography by John D. Weigand
Poetry by Penelope Dyan

There are so many things
in New Orleans
that you can find to do
And when YOU get to New Orleans,
what you do up to YOU!
You could take a swamp tour,
but who knows?
Mom says, "A gator just MIGHT
bite off YOUR nose!"
Then, because your two sisters
burst into tantrum-like screams,
Dad says, "Let's visit the site of
the Battle of New Orleans!"

RIVER CRUISES

Paddlewheeler Creole Queen

Battlefield Cruise
Narrated Cruise to Chalmette Battlefield
2 Hour 30 Minute Cruise

Jazz Dinner Cruise
Live Music, Creole Cajun Dinner Buffet
2 Hour Cruise

TOURS
- City Tours
- Plantation Tours
- Ghost • Vampire Voodoo Tours

For Information on all tours or to make reservations:
504.529.456

PLEASE...
No Outside Beve[rages]
Food Allowed
Thank You

Jean Lafitte Swamp Tours Airboat Tours

A Real Swamp Adventure!
Only 25 Minutes From Here
Large & Small Airboats
Swamp Tour: 1 Hour 30 Minutes
Airboat Tour: 1 Hour 45 Minutes

River Cruises | **TOURS**

Then you all hop aboard
the Creole Queen,
and you go off to see
what STILL can be seen.
Your sister, Sally, says,
"You must be REALLY nuts,
if you THINK you'll see
lots of old bones and dried guts!"
You know your sister isn't wrong;
and that sadly, all THAT gross stuff
is long ago gone!

You arrive right at the dock.
The stage is all set.
You say to your sis,
"This will be the most fun yet!"
Your two sisters look at you,
and they shake their heads.
It's the long, long walk
from the boat,
that they most dread.
(But they're just girls,
and they won't last long.)
And you're a boy, big and strong!

Everyone leaves the boat.
You start to walk.
And on the way,
people start to talk.
This is the place of the LAST battle
of the War of 1812, it seems,
seven miles down the Mississippi
from the city of New Orleans.

To the old plantation house you walk;
and you are quiet, and you don't talk.
You think about the history
of this fine old place,
as you continue to walk
at an even pace.
Bought by two brothers
who were legally declared
'free men of color'
way back in 1817,
they restored the house and fields
of sugarcane green!

You continue to walk along
yet another long path.
Mom says she's tired and needs a bath.
You are full of energy,
as happy as any boy could possibly be!
Your two sisters continue to complain.
You decide they're crazy
and that they're just a pain.
Your dad just smiles down at you,
because (after all) what's a dad to do?

Mom finds a place to rest
at a picnic table right under a tree.
You see something not far ahead,
and then you shout, "Yippee!"
You sisters look up at you
and roll their eyes.
Their annoyance with
their big brother,
they just CAN'T disguise!

You see some cannons!
They're all lined up in a row!
You declare,
"Now, that is the next place
that I want to go!"
And so you get up and RUN
toward that cannon of black and red,
with visions of smoking
cannonballs firing,
racing straight through YOUR head!

Then to the back of THIS cannon
and to its cannonballs you run!
Your mom shouts,
"Don't YOU touch anything!"
And she spoils all YOUR fun!
So you use your imagination.
(You pretend you are defending
your nation.)
YOU are Andrew Jackson
fighting alongside the pirate,
Jean Lafitte;
And the thought of THAT,
is REALLY neat!

Next, you see a tree.
It's PERFECT for a swing!
You imagine ALL the happiness
a swing like THAT could bring.
Your sisters imagine just sitting there,
as YOU happily imagine
flying right through the air!
You think,
"That tree, like me, is one of a kind."
Your mother seems to read your mind.
She says,
"I know you want to climb that tree,
but don't YOU dare!
You're not going anywhere!"

You look out at the battlefield
and see MORE trees of green.
You try to imagine the battle scene.
And you are fascinated that battle lasted so long,
as the battle for freedom
went on and on,
as from 1814 into 1815, it seems,
soldiers fought the long, bloody
Battle of New Orleans!

You think about all of those bodies,
and all of that blood,
that must have laid right there
in the water and in the mud,
as you stare down
at the puddles in the grass so green,
just down the Mississippi,
down in New Orleans

And then when the day
at the battle site is finally all done,
you decide YOU have had
a whole LOT of fun!
And as on two backs
your two sisters piggyback ride,
you decide to walk;
because you're strong inside!
You walk, even though now,
you have VERY sore feet,
and all YOU want to DO is eat and eat!

"To the victors belong the spoils."

Andrew Jackson
The Seventh President of the United States of America

Neither wind, nor sleet nor snow, rain or heat, can stop a strong, curious, or hungry boy!"

Penelope Dyan

www.ingramcontent.com/pod-product-compliance
Ingram Content Group UK Ltd.
Pitfield, Milton Keynes, MK11 3LW, UK
UKHW060136240426
12048UKWH00002B/58